Smart Animals

PIGS

by Duncan Searl

Consultant: Karl Kranz
General Curator
The Maryland Zoo in Baltimore

BEARPORT
PUBLISHING COMPANY, INC.

New York, New York

Credits

Cover (background), Fielding Peipereit/istockphoto; Cover (center), Kevin Russ/istockphoto; Title Page, Kevin Russ/istockphoto; 4, Dennis Light/Light Photographic; 5, Houston Chronicle; 6, Pittsburgh Post Gazette; 7, AP Wide World Photos; 8, Jeff Greenberg/Omni; 9, Gay Bamgamer/Alamy; 10, Paul M. Thompson/Alamy; 11, Grant Heilman; 12, Howard Nuernberger/Penn State College of Agricultural Science; 13, George D. Lepp/Corbis; 14, Arthur C. Smith/Grant Heilmant; 15, E.A. Janes/age fotostock/SuperStock; 16, Scott Sinklier/AGStock USA, Inc./Alamy; 17, Richard K. Balsbaugh, University of Illinois; 18, Bruce Barbey/Magnum Photos; 18 (inset), Steven Rothfield/Getty Images; 19, Dennis Light/Light Photographic; 20, Ron Cash; 21, Ron Cash; 22, Lynn Stone; 23, AP Wide World Photos; 24 (map), Dave Herring; 24 (top), G.W. Willis/Animals Animals/Earth Scenes; 24 (bottom), Studio Carlo Dani/Animals Animals/Earth Scenes; 25, Paul Glendell/Peter Arnold; 26, AP Wide World Photos; 27, IFA Bilderteam/eStock Photo; 28 (left), Royalty Free; 28 (right), Gay Bamgamer/Alamy; 29, AP Wide World Photos.

Special thanks to Dr. Stanley Curtis, Department of Animal Sciences, University of Illinois, Urbana

Design and production by Dawn Beard Creative and Octavo Design and Production, Inc.

Library of Congress Cataloging-in-Publication Data

Searl, Duncan.
  Pigs / by Duncan Searl.
    p. cm.—(Smart animals!)
  Includes bibliographical references and index.
  ISBN-13: 978-1-59716-164-0 (library binding)
  ISBN-10: 1-59716-164-0 (library binding)
  1. Swine—Juvenile literature. 2. Animal intelligence—Juvenile literature. I. Title. II. Series.

  SF395.5.S43 2006
  636.4—dc22

                       2005026827

For more information, write to Bearport Publishing Company, Inc., 101 Fifth Avenue, Suite 6R, New York, New York 10003. Printed in the United States of America.

10 9 8 7 6 5 4 3 2

 # Contents

Priscilla to the Rescue

Anthony was in trouble. The 11-year-old Texas boy had swum too far out in the lake. Suddenly, the water was over his head, and he began to **panic**. He screamed for help.

Pigs are strong swimmers. Like people, they love the water in hot weather.

Fortunately, Priscilla had come to the lake that same day. She was enjoying a swim when she heard the screams. Priscilla quickly paddled toward Anthony. Somehow, the drowning boy stayed afloat until she reached him. Then he grabbed onto Priscilla and she pulled him to safety.

People on the **shore** watched in amazement. Priscilla the pig was a hero!

▲ **Priscilla was only about two months old when she saved Anthony. She was honored with a "Priscilla the Pig Day" in Houston, Texas.**

Life-Saving Pigs

Priscilla was smart enough to see that Anthony needed help. She also figured out how to help him. Her actions wouldn't surprise many people who keep pigs as pets.

Jo Ann Altsman owes her life to her potbellied pet pig, Lulu. When Jo Ann collapsed from a heart attack, Lulu knew something was wrong. So she walked outside and headed toward the road. Lulu had never been there before.

▲ **Lulu**

A car soon came down the road. Lulu lay down in front of it. When the driver stopped and got out, Lulu led him into the house. Minutes later, an emergency crew was at the scene.

In the 1970s and 1980s, potbellied pigs were brought from Vietnam to be shown in zoos. People liked them so much that they began to keep them as pets.

▲ Jo Ann and her heroic pig, who was being honored in New York

Sheep Dogs and Sheep Pigs

Everyone knows dogs are smart, but are pigs even smarter? Some people think so. Many pigs can learn anything that dogs can—and in less time.

Katy Cropper, a sheep dog trainer, worked with pigs. She taught pigs to round up sheep and split them into smaller groups. Those are the same jobs that sheep dogs do.

Like dogs, pigs learn their names when they are two or three weeks old and come when they are called.

Others have trained pigs to help the blind. Unlike **seeing-eye dogs**, seeing-eye pigs never chase cats or other animals. Pigs also stand out in a crowd. So people notice them—and the blind people they're leading.

▲ **In addition to herding sheep, pigs have been trained to hunt. Pigs can silently point in the direction of the hunted animal, just like dogs.**

Amazing Pigs

Finding the way through a **maze** is one sign of **intelligence**. Scientists at Cornell University in New York set up several large mazes. They wanted to see how quickly different animals could get through them.

▲ **This pig is moving through an obstacle course.**

Dogs scored well on the maze test. Chickens and horses got through it, too, but they took longer than dogs. Sheep never made it through, and cats refused to take part in the **experiments**.

Pigs, however, scored the highest! They made it through the maze first every time. Scientists think pigs scored well because they are good at solving problems.

Pigs use their **keen** ears and noses to gather information. Their eyes, which are similar to people's, are fairly sharp, too.

Ping-Pong Pigs

Professor Stanley Curtis also studies pig intelligence. In one experiment, he compared how well pigs and chimps were able to learn a new game.

▼ **Dr. Curtis used video games to figure out how smart pigs are.**

Chimps had been taught to play a computer game like Ping-Pong. They had moved joysticks with their hands to hit targets on a screen. So Dr. Curtis taught pigs to play the same game. Yet there was one big difference. The pigs used their **snouts** to move the joysticks. How did they do? It turned out that pigs learned the game as quickly as chimps.

◀ A pig's snout is both tough and sensitive. Muscles move the snout up, down, and back to express the pig's moods.

Pigs are easy to train. They learn to walk on leashes more quickly than dogs.

Pig Talk

Computer games are only the beginning for Dr. Curtis. His long-term goal is to figure out the meaning of pig squeals and grunts. Then it might be possible to **communicate** with pigs.

Pigs "talk" constantly with one another. So far, scientists have learned the meaning of more than 20 of their sounds. *Baawrp*, for example, means a pig is happy.

▲ **Pigs are social animals. They enjoy close contact with other pigs and with people.**

Pigs communicate with songs, too. A mother pig, or **sow**, sings a special song to her **piglets** when **nursing**. She sings another song to her **mate**.

▲ **Pigs are excellent mothers. A giant sow takes special care not to crush her tiny babies.**

Pigs have large **litters**. The average size is 8 to 12 piglets, but one sow had a litter of 37!

Hot and Cold Pigs

Most pigs in the United States live in large sheds with many **pens**. Sometimes the **temperature** in these pens gets too hot or too cold for the pigs. So some **animal biologists** have looked for ways to help farm animals make themselves more comfortable.

Some pigs were taught to control the temperatures in their pens. When the pigs were too hot, they used their snouts to push a switch. Then the temperature would go down. The pigs were able to cool off. The animals were smart enough to help run their own farms!

▲ **These pigs used their snouts to turn on heat lamps when they were cold.**

Pigs have been trained to turn the lights on in their pens when it gets dark. When it's too bright, they turn them off.

Truffle Sniffers

Training pigs to do jobs is nothing new. In France, trained pigs have been digging up truffles for hundreds of years.

A truffle is a delicious and rare kind of mushroom. Some truffles sell for $1,000 a pound (.5 kg)! They're expensive because they grow underground and are very hard to find.

Truffles ▶

▲ **This man hunts truffles with a trained pig. Over 2,000 years ago, ancient Romans also used pigs to hunt for truffles.**

That's where the pigs come in. With their keen sense of smell, pigs can sniff out truffles under the soil. Then they use their snouts like shovels to **root** them out.

Pigs love truffles as much as people do. So the handlers have to train the pigs not to gobble down the truffles they dig up.

If a pig nuzzles a plastic playing card, his keen nose can pick that card from a pack several days later, even after the cards have been washed.

▲ **Rooting in the ground comes naturally to a pig, even when there are no truffles. So pet pig owners must often choose between pigs and flower gardens.**

Police Pig

If pigs can sniff out truffles, can they find **illegal** drugs, too? That's what the police in Portland, Oregon, wanted to know. So they put Harley, a potbellied piglet, on the force.

Sniffing drugs is usually a dog's job. Trying to use a pig made sense, though. First, pigs have keener noses than dogs. They are also easier to train. In addition, little Harley only weighed 40 pounds (18 kg). So he was easy to feed and care for.

Officer
Ron Cash and Harley   **1994**

Potbellied pigs aren't fast and athletic like dogs. So Harley's trainer had to carry the pig sometimes. To make friends with his partner, the trainer even learned to grunt!

Harley was such a success that the Portland Police decided to train pigs to sniff for guns.

As Clean as a Pig

In hot weather, pigs like to roll in mud. Yet they don't enjoy being dirty. They're just trying to find a way to stay cool.

Unlike people, pigs aren't able to sweat to cool their bodies. So they lie in cool places. If there's no water around, mud will do.

Pigs are very sensitive to heat. Direct sunlight on a hot day that is over 80°F (27°C) can kill a pig.

Actually, pigs are quite clean. Pet pigs, for example, quickly learn to use a **litter box**. On farms, pigs set aside one small area as a bathroom. The rest of the pen is their living space. Keeping clean in these ways is smart. It helps a pig stay healthy.

▲ **On hot days, pigs lie in mud or water to avoid overheating.**

Smart, Wild Cousins

Although farm pigs are smart, their wild cousins are even smarter. Some scientists believe that's because they need to use their brains more.

Wild pigs have to think about how to find food in the forest or jungle. They have to escape from their enemies, too.

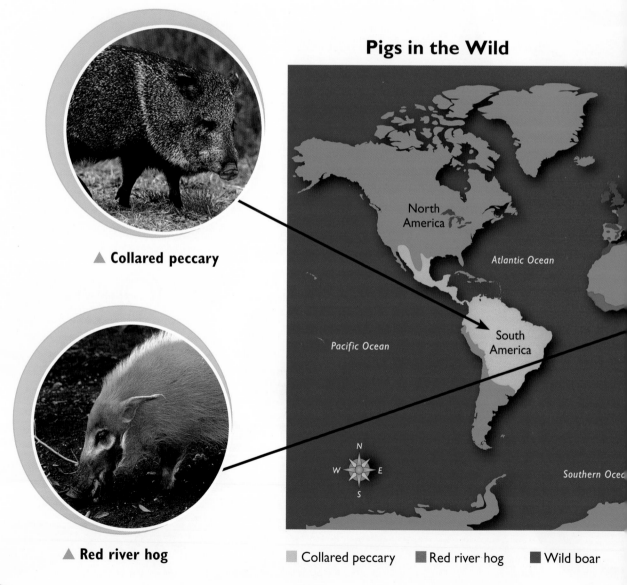

▲ **Collared peccary**

▲ **Red river hog**

Pigs in the Wild

North America

Atlantic Ocean

Pacific Ocean

South America

Southern Ocea

N
W E
S

■ Collared peccary   ■ Red river hog   ■ Wild boar

On large farms, pigs don't have to solve these problems. They spend most of their time sleeping and eating. So, over the years, their brains have gotten 20 percent smaller.

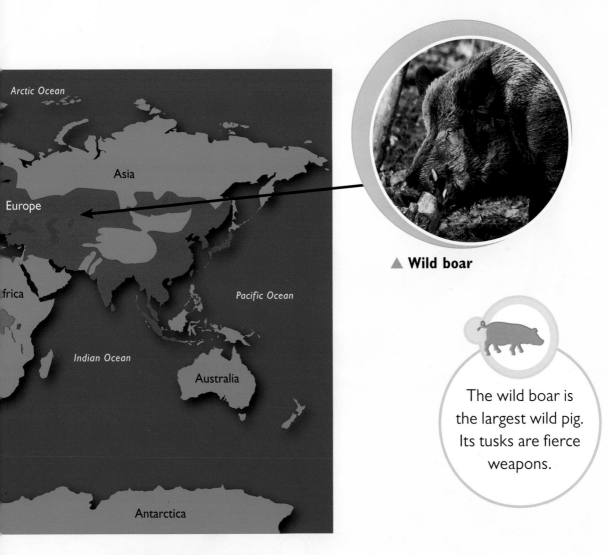

▲ **Wild boar**

The wild boar is the largest wild pig. Its tusks are fierce weapons.

▲ **This map shows where some wild pigs live.**

Pigs and People

People first **domesticated** pigs about 10,000 years ago. Since then, wild pigs have been domesticated many times and in many places. In fact, pigs can be found on almost every continent on Earth.

People have trained pigs to guard their property when they are away.

Yet no matter where pigs live, one thing stays the same. Whether in the wild, on farms, or in homes, pigs still surprise people with their intelligence and brainy behavior.

▲ Pigs, like dogs, respond well to people who show them respect and affection.

Just the Facts

	Domesticated Farm Pig	Potbellied Pig

Weight	300–500 pounds (136–227 kg)	90–150 pounds (41–68 kg)
Length	4–6 feet (1.2–1.8 m)	3 feet (.9 m)
Height	2–3 feet (.6–.9 m)	1½–2 feet (.5–.6 m)
Life Span	9–15 years	10–15 years
Average Litter Size	8–12 piglets	4–12 piglets

More Smart Pigs

In Scotland, a 250-pound (113-kg) boar named McQueen escaped a butcher by leaping over a six-foot (2-m) wall. For days, he dodged the men who chased him. Eventually, McQueen found a home on a friendly farm.

On a farm in Chico, California, Spammy the pig shared a shed with her friend, Spot the calf. When a fire broke out, Spammy found a way to save them. She smashed a hole in the wall so that the two of them could escape to safety.

◀ **Spammy and Spot**

Glossary

animal biologists
(AN-uh-muhl bye-OL-uh-jists)
scientists who study animals

communicate
(kuh-MYOO-nuh-kate) to pass on
facts, ideas, thoughts, or feelings

domesticated
(duh-MESS-tuh-*kate*-id) bred and
tamed animals for use by humans

experiments (ek-SPER-uh-ments)
scientific tests that are set up to find
the answer to a question

illegal (i-LEE-guhl) against the law

intelligence (in-TEL-uh-juhns)
the ability to learn and understand,
or to solve problems

keen (KEEN) very sensitive

litter box (LIT-ur BOKS) a box
filled with clay, sand, or other
material, and used by pets as a place
to go to the bathroom

litters (LIT-urz) all of the young
born at one time to a mammal

mate (MATE) a male or female
partner

maze (MAYZ) a confusing series
of winding paths that is hard to find
a way through

nursing (NURSS-ing) feeding young
with a mother's milk

panic (PAN-ik) feel very afraid

pens (PENZ) small enclosed areas
for animals, such as pigs, sheep, and
cows

piglets (PIG-lits) young pigs

root (ROOT) using a snout to dig
up things in the ground

seeing-eye dogs
(SEE-ing-EYE DOGZ) dogs that are
trained to help and guide blind people

shore (SHOR) the land along the
edge of a lake, river, or ocean

snouts (SNOUTS) the long, front
part of an animal's head that sticks
out; it includes the nose, and usually
the jaws and mouth as well

sow (SOU) a female adult pig

temperature (TEM-pur-uh-chur)
how hot or cold something is

Bibliography

Balliet, Gay L. *Lowell: The True Story of an Existential Pig.* Far Hills, NJ: New Horizon Press (2000).

Bonera, Franco. *Pigs: Art, Legend, History.* Boston: Bullfinch Press (1991).

Nissenson, Marilyn, and Susan Jonas. *The Ubiquitous Pig.* New York: Harry N. Abrams (1996).

Rath, Sara. *The Complete Pig: An Entertaining History of Pigs of the World.* Stillwater, MN: Voyageur Press (2004).

Watson, Lyall. *The Whole Hog: Exploring the Extraordinary Potential of Pigs.* Washington, D.C.: Smithsonian Books (2004).

Read More

Miller, Sara Swan. *Pigs.* Danbury, CT: Children's Press (2000).

Schmidt, Annemarie. *Pigs and Peccaries.* Milwaukee, WI: Gareth Stevens Publishing (1994).

Scott, Jack Denton. *The Book of the Pig.* New York: Putnam (1981).

Learn More Online

Visit these Web sites to learn more about pigs:

www.nationalgeographic.com/kids/creature_feature/0106/
   warthogs.html

www.pbs.org/wnet/nature/pigs

Index

About the Author

Duncan Searl is a writer and editor who lives in New York. He is the author of many books for young readers.